An Americ␣␣ of Cul␣

THE CARNEGIE INSTITUTE AND CARNEGIE LIBRARY OF PITTSBURGH

by James D. Van Trump

*with foreword by James M. Walton
and introduction by Charles Covert Arensburg*

PUBLISHED BY
CARNEGIE INSTITUTE
AND
PITTSBURGH HISTORY & LANDMARKS FOUNDATION
PITTSBURGH, PENNSYLVANIA

Dedicated to

STANTON BELFOUR

A fine historian and a friend of Pittsburgh

CONTENTS

First Forbes Avenue entrance of Carnegie Music Hall, 1895

FOREWORD

I believe it is fitting at this time to remember the past of Carnegie Institute and Carnegie Library of Pittsburgh, as we think and plan for the future.

Andrew Carnegie was ever farsighted in his view of Pittsburgh and wanted it not only to be the steel capital of the world but to provide a stimulating cultural environment for the people who live in the area. He was interested in bringing here the finest in art, music, and literature; he was a leader in realizing the importance of natural history in the life of man. He wanted these things to be available to the people with whom he made his fortune.

He was not only interested in what was going on in his day but realized that growth must come with the future. Commenting in 1899 on the plans for expanding the Institute and Library, he wrote: "You will notice that the proposed extension will bring the building to Mawhinney Street. It would seem advisable for the city, when it is condemning ground, to embrace some distance beyond that street, because if the past history of the Institute proves anything, it is that continual growth is the law of its being."

Today we are growing. We have acquired the property on the other side of Mawhinney Street, and are in the process of planning a new Museum of Art building generously given by the Scaife family in memory of Sarah Mellon Scaife. In the spirit of Andrew Carnegie we are expanding inwardly and outwardly, to continue providing a cultural center for the people of Pittsburgh and surrounding areas.

It is our hope that by publishing this book jointly with the Pittsburgh History & Landmarks Foundation we may set down for history the beginning and bring to light some of the architectural details of the building that Andrew Carnegie considered one of the most important accomplishments of his life—a building that has maintained its place in the lives of several generations of Pittsburghers.

We are remembering the past with this book and at the same time are looking to the future to carry on a tradition.

James M. Walton

JAMES M. WALTON
PRESIDENT
CARNEGIE INSTITUTE

Overall view of Carnegie Institute from Forbes Avenue, 1902

INTRODUCTION

*"The most beautiful thing we can experience is the mysterious.
It is the source of all true art and science."*
ALBERT EINSTEIN 1930

This book really began over fifteen years ago when James D. Van Trump, well known for his research and publications on the architectural history of Pittsburgh, began to examine the history of the Carnegie Institute building. As he compiled his research he wrote a series of articles on the development, the architecture, and the community significance of Carnegie Institute, which were published between 1957 and 1965 in *Carnegie Magazine.*

The Pittsburgh History & Landmarks Foundation felt that his research deserved a wider audience and more permanent form because Carnegie Institute is an extraordinary structure in the cultural and architectural history of the United States in that it houses the main city library, a museum of natural history, a music hall and a department of fine arts under one roof. Through the years it has also become part of the fiber of our community because it serves as custodian of the cultural heritage of mankind for this city.

The officers of Carnegie Institute also felt that the history of the building should be recorded in book form and made available to the public and to scholars interested in American cultural history and museum development.

Together we applied to the Pittsburgh Foundation for funds to finance rewriting the original articles and augmenting them with considerable pictorial material. The Melissa S. McKee Carnahan Trust of the Pittsburgh Foundation made the funds available.

Jeannette F. Seneff, associate editor of *Carnegie Magazine,* and Arthur P. Ziegler, Jr., our executive director, carried out the editorial work, and Mr. Ziegler coordinated the project. Art and design were under the direction of A. H. Kiefer.

CHARLES COVERT ARENSBERG
PRESIDENT
PITTSBURGH HISTORY &
LANDMARKS FOUNDATION

IX

Overall view in 1902 showing future site of Schenley Plaza
Carnegie Institute, April 1907, showing bridge now buried

I

A PALATIAL IMAGE FOR THE PEOPLE

The Architecture of
the Carnegie Institute Building

SQUARE AND FORTHRIGHT, massive and expansively domed, the grey bulk of the Carnegie Institute, covering nearly five acres of ground, looms and presides as Pittsburgh's prime symbol of culture among the towers of Oakland.

Midway between the soaring height of the Cathedral of Learning and the spreading horizontality of the Carnegie-Mellon University, it separates and to some extent confines the two building groups; culturally it supplements and serves them both. First opened in 1895 and much expanded in 1904-07, it is of considerable interest as a monument of late-nineteenth-century cultural idealism, and it still represents to all Pittsburghers, in this frenetic and televisioned day, the graces and the serenities of an elder time.

This combination of library, art gallery, natural history museum, and music hall illustrates, probably better than any other example in America, the attempt to concentrate a number of cultural functions under one roof in line with much nineteenth-century practice.

A noble experiment, a gracious reminder of one stage in our cultural development, it solidly remains a palace of culture and a servant of the people for whom it was intended. The benefactions of nineteenth-century philanthropists like Andrew Carnegie were not infrequently enormous and commensurate with the fortunes they had gained, but they were intended primarily to serve the great body of the people, the middle and lower classes especially. They were, therefore, democratic in both scale and purpose.

If the tone of Andrew Carnegie's donations to Pittsburgh's cultural life was democratic, the form of his buildings was palatial. Carnegie Institute was intended as a cultural palace—for the people. In Europe, as monarchs and royal governments vanished, their palaces —the structural archetypes associated with culture—were taken over by the rising democratic regimes and devoted to cultural activities. In America, where there were no vacated palaces, new museums and art galleries—imitating European models—were conceived in the old palatial mold. The Carnegie Institute buildings were not exceptional in this respect, and thus it was that the spirit of Versailles and the

Louvre, transformed and popularized, arose again, among the industrial hills of Pittsburgh.

It was practically received opinion in the new democratic world that cultural development was one of the legitimate goals of Everyman, and it was the job of the architect to make the instruments of that development easily available. The building must be located at some central place convenient to the largest number of people; the books must be consulted or the objects looked upon in the easiest and most efficient manner. These were primary considerations for the architects of the first Carnegie building, and in so far as the palace type did not meet the new requirements, it had to be modified. The building type represented by the Carnegie Institute is related to the department store, the union railroad station, and the hotel. In the greatest cities of the Western world it was usual, even in our period, to construct the library, art gallery, or museum as separate buildings, but in the smaller provincial towns of England and France the tripartite combination was fairly common. What makes the Pittsburgh building so uniquely interesting is the addition of yet another element—the music hall.

There is, therefore, a certain provincial, almost a parochial, quality implicit in the original conception of the Carnegie Institute building, underlined by the fact that Andrew Carnegie considered his cultural institutions as essentially community centers. To some degree, the prototype of both the Allegheny Library (dedicated 1890) and the Pittsburgh structure may be found in the first of his American libraries to be opened to the public—that of Braddock, Pennsylvania, (a paternalistic venture directly benefiting his own workmen) which was dedicated in 1889 and had not only a collection of books and historical relics, but also an auditorium, gymnasium, and social hall. The theme was continued in his later Pittsburgh branch libraries, which were usually provided with an auditorium. The recreational facilities of Braddock were not included in either the Allegheny or Pittsburgh projects, but the idea is the same, no matter how different the scale. At Pittsburgh, the Braddock workmen's clubhouse has monumentally become the urban citizen's palace for cultural recreation.

As early as 1881 Andrew Carnegie had offered the City of Pittsburgh $250,000 for the erection of a public library building with the stipulation, however, that the municipality maintain it, but the offer was not at that time accepted. In 1890, the prospective donor made a second offer, of a million dollars to erect a structure that would house not only a library but also art galleries, a museum, headquarters for learned societies, and a concert hall. The city ordinance accepting this offer was passed in May, 1890, and a board of trustees was formed consisting of a number of prominent Pittsburgh men. In 1891 the City authorized the Board to construct the new building at the main entrance of the Schenley Park tract. This land was contiguous to Oakland, a part of the city equidistant from "downtown" and from the great residential section of East Liberty, as well as a district that already seemed destined to become the municipal civic center.

Foundation of the Carnegie Institute in Oakland so eminently established and enthroned the cultural tone that most of the city's similar activities were attracted to the same spot, including two institutions of learning.

Shortly after the Board of Trustees was formed, an invitation was issued to all architects to submit drawings in competition for the new building. Architectural competitions were accepted practice in the late-nineteenth century, and ninety-seven American architects exhibited one hundred and two sets of drawings in Pittsburgh—the largest exhibition of the sort ever held in America up to that time. After some consideration the Board accepted the plans of Longfellow, Alden and Harlow, a firm that had offices in both Boston and Pittsburgh. The foundation was finished in 1892, and the completed structure was dedicated on November 5, 1895.

The artistic ancestry of the firm who designed the first Institute is of great importance in any consideration of the structure's form and style. With the advent of the great H. H. Richardson (1838-86) in Pittsburgh, the city entered on a new phase architecturally, a greater maturity of practice and outlook. Richardson's Allegheny County Buildings (1884-88) represent locally a sort of dividing line between an earlier stylistic provincialism and the full tide of late-nineteenth-century Eclecticism.

At that time the main style currents, particularly the Richardsonian Romanesque and the new Classicism, were flowing in strongly from the East, especially from New England, and Pittsburgh's constructional climate was to a great degree affected by them. Not only Richardson himself, but some of his disciples were responsible for this transition. The most important of them, Frank E. Alden (1859-1908), who had been in Richardson's Boston office, came here in 1885 as supervising architect on the County Buildings, and with him the New England influence was firmly established. In 1887 he with two other new Englanders, A. W. Longfellow (1854-1934) and A. B. Harlow (1857-1927), formed the firm of Longfellow, Alden and Harlow. Longfellow, who managed the Boston office, withdrew in 1896, just after the first Carnegie building was finished, and it was the reconstituted firm of Alden and Harlow that gave the structure its final shape in 1904-07.

It was the 1891 Carnegie commission, however, that set up the architects for two decades as the pre-eminent practioners of their art in Pittsburgh—the local equivalent of the nationally known firm of McKim, Mead and White. The latter office had a reputation for taste (chiefly Classical), and a taste for palaces—and in this regard the local firm was not far behind them. Carnegie Institute in its present form is certainly the chef-d'oeuvre of its architects, and after the Allegheny County Buildings it remains one of the chief monuments of the late Eclectic period in Pittsburgh.

The first Carnegie building was also the earliest large example in Pittsburgh of the new Classical manner, based for the most part on the earlier Italian Renaissance, which was being enthusiastically developed by McKim, Mead and White. Boston Public Library designed by that firm in 1888 was one of the most important American buildings of the nineteenth century, and it profoundly influenced our building in both form and style. Longfellow, Alden and Harlow harked back to Friedrich von Gärtner's Royal Library (1832-43) at Munich, whose early Florentine *palazzo* mass and detailing may have provided the model for our structure; the Institute, however, makes use of a slightly later stylistic version of the quattrocento theme.

Like the Boston Library, the Pittsburgh building had a rusticated lower story, but the large mullioned windows of the second floor (the Italian *piano nobile*) echo the fenestration of Florentine palaces. Imitated also from Boston are the triple arches of the main entrance with their large scrolled keystones, but the Corinthian peristyle above the entry is an unhappy feature added in 1904-07. Italianate again was the roof of red tiles, a feature that disappeared with the remodeling, but which, for the term of its existence, proved a pleasant foil to the grey sandstone walls.

The general tone of the Pittsburgh work is quiet and correct, but there are details like the paneled attic that exhibit a certain provincial awkwardness. Not so accomplished or so learned a piece of work as Boston, there is implicit, nonetheless, in the Pittsburgh structure, that same cool elegance, that beguiling reflection and translation of the miraculous quattrocento tone, that seems to have flowered anew among our clouded hills.

The original Carnegie building rather noticeably, but not too forcibly, divided into two parts: the library-art gallery-museum structure, a H-shaped parallelogram facing the park entrance; and the Music Hall, a semicircular auditorium with two towers, the main entrance to which was on Forbes Avenue. We have here, also, two types of architectural composition—the new and fashionable horizontality of the Library mass and the uneven Romantic outline of the Hall, which had been so modish in the High Victorian period. Separation of function was expressed on the exterior of the library section by the projection of the lateral wings, one of which was occupied by the art gallery and the other by the museum. Considering the many activities that had to be housed in the whole structure, the architects may be said to have successfully managed the amalgamation of function.

The first version of the Music Hall introduces the palatial note again, but in another sense—that of the nineteenth-century exhibition building, which itself is yet another extension of the palace motif into the new democratic age. The idea of expressing the semicircular form of the theater on the exterior of the building seems to have been chiefly advanced by the Germans.

However, the immediate prototype of our half circle with the two towers, one at each side, was undoubtedly the Palais du Trocadéro designed by Davioud and Bourdais for the Paris Exposition of 1878, for many years one of the familiar sights of Paris. There is also a design by Sir Rowand Anderson, published in the *Building News* of 1879, for the McEwan Hall of Edinburgh University, which, especially in the tower treatment, may have influenced the Pittsburgh project. Despite the quattrocento detailing and the Romantic outline, the disposition of the mass is largely neo-Baroque.

The two towers, rather tame but pleasant versions of the Campanile of San Marco at Venice, were the dominant vertical accents in the general composition and served notably to distract the eye from that point where the Music Hall joined the rest of the structure. These ornamental campanili whose belfries sheltered neither bell nor watchman ceased to enliven the Oakland scene after 1904; many years later they rose again in another reincarnation — the great skyscraper university across the street.

The interior plan of the whole building was, in the main, well articulated and adequate to the proper functioning of the various parts not only separately but in conjunction with one another. Tuscan-vaulted transverse corridors on both the first and the second floors of the library section connected the art and science wings, and the quattrocento vistas they created formed an architecturally poetic link between the rather Baroque galleries of the one and the more utilitarian display rooms of the other. They are still extant, but they now serve merely to connect various portions of the library.

Each part of the structure had its separate entrance, but the most important of these was the central entry, whose groined vaults and severely treated pilasters recall the vestibule of the Boston Public Library and also, curiously enough, the Romanesque staircase hall of the Allegheny County Court House. The stairs here were neither well inte-

5

grated into the general plan nor adequate, because the main flight rose directly into the Reference Reading Room—a serious fault that was corrected when the present handsome double stairway of Tennessee marble was erected in 1904-07.

The main lending room on the first floor is still used as such, but it is much changed, although the tripartite division of the forepart has not been extensively altered: what were once two periodical reading rooms are now the Public Affairs Room and the Gillespie Room. The dividing arcades with their Palladian arches are unchanged, but the quattro-cento hooded fireplaces of red Verona marble that contributed so eminently to the Florentine palatial note are gone. How elegantly and yet forlornly these monumental chimney pieces, empty of fire and purpose, lingered in Eclectic rooms such as these; mere ornamental survivors, they were sacrificed in the end to utilitarian aims.

At the back of the room lay the entrance to the first version of the "stack" wing—a storeroom, absolutely necessary in any modern library, which in this instance formed a smaller projection between the art and the science sections. This structure, with six floors and 3,500 running feet of shelf space, became increasingly inadequate as the book collection increased, and now it serves merely as a vestibule to the present larger stack erected in 1904.

In the great Reference Reading Room on the second floor of the library, the magnificence of Rome was made manifest in late-Victorian Pittsburgh. The architects of the quattrocento and the Renaissance generally had never ceased to be haunted by Roman grandeur, and the later men of the nineteenth century, driven by the necessity of creating great halls, looked back upon the baths and basilicas of the Imperial City—looked back and were caught up in the antique dream of column and vault. The engineers had other solutions to such programs of construction, but they were not regarded as "artistic." For the huge reading rooms of the new democratic libraries, contemporary architects used either the tunnel-vaulted gallery or the domed rotunda. McKim, Mead and White had provided the gallery model in the long vaulted reference room of the Boston library—imitated, in the idea at least, by Carrere and Hastings at the New York Public Library (1902-10). The Boston model was reproduced closely, but rather more simply, in the Pittsburgh gallery, which, with its ample dimensions (91 feet long, 44 feet wide, and 30 feet high), its coffered tunnel-vault, and its gilded fifteenth-century detailing was, and still is, one of the handsomest rooms in the whole building.

To awe-struck Pittsburghers of the nineties, so unused to having Classical galleries in their midst, it was little short of a vision; it was the "grand gold hall", a wonder and eminently a sign of a new splendor available to all the people. Undoubtedly it prepared the way for the more sumptuous Parisian elegance of the Music Hall Foyer.

Several of the chief rooms of the library, the vestibule, and the two transverse corridors were chastely and simply decorated with frescoes. Some of these still survive, notably the publisher's colophons and printer's marks on the walls of the lending and reference rooms and the painted decorations of the Music Hall. Much of this work was executed by Elmer Ellsworth Garnsey (1862-1946), who had assisted in the decoration of both the Boston Public Library and the Library of Congress. The architects of these great nineteenth-century palaces and their patrons often called in other artists as coworkers, thus reviving under democratic auspices the old Renaissance conception of the interdependence of the arts.

The interior of the Music Hall, unchanged by the rebuilding of 1904-07, still retains its original decorative flavor and its rich color scheme of white, gold, and dull rose-red. The auditorium with its two galleries seats a little more than 2,000 people and has not only the amplitude and openness of the new democratic theater form but also some of the grace and intimacy of the eighteenth-century playhouse.

The coffered half-dome of the ceiling echoes the Roman Pantheon, providing yet another instance of haunting Roman forms, although it is probable that this vault was inspired by eighteenth-century models. Again, the quattrocento note is much in evidence in the delicate gilded arabesques of the proscenium and the treatment of the organ case above the stage, whose colonnettes and garlands have the charming youthful freshness of the great Florentine century. The four stage boxes of the proscenium, which again recall eighteenth-century practice, seem more architectural than social adjuncts; the almost complete absence of the loge in this hall proclaims most distinctly the egalitarian note.

The Music Hall served and still serves Everyman, and its quiet but elegant decorative scheme has been a background not only for the evening toilettes of the more prosperous classes, but also for the "Sunday best" of the workingmen families who came to hear the organ concerts.

For many years after it was opened in 1895, the Music Hall was the center of Pittsburgh musical activity. The Art Society founded in 1873 held its concerts here from 1896 until it suspended its activities in 1943, and from 1896 until 1910 the hall was the home of the first Pittsburgh Symphony. The free organ recitals instituted at the express wish of Andrew Carnegie, held weekly since 1895 and monthly during the winter since 1966, have been a notably democratic factor in Pittsburgh musical life. In 1925 the trustees of Carnegie Institute, in an effort to retain concert engagements that were moving to larger halls, wished to enlarge the auditorium by moving the stage wall backward, but nothing

7

came of the project. Although it is not the largest concert hall in Pittsburgh, it still functions admirably and has a very active schedule during the concert season.

It is to be hoped that the Music Hall will never be changed, because a great part of its charm lies in its intimacy and its relative smallness as well as in the memories it harbors. The most famous musical artists of the last sixty years have performed in the Music Hall.

In the present Carnegie Institute the cultural palace reached huge and opulent dimensions quite in keeping with the expansive and prosperous period at the turn of the century. The rebuilding of 1904-07 gave quite another appearance to the structure—the thin elegance of the old work was incorporated, heavily embraced, in the new additions that exemplified not only the might and pride of the Western democratic world, but also the achievements and munificence of Andrew Carnegie, who was so eminently a product of that world.

The huge late-Victorian and Edwardian expositions and fairs—showcases for the wealth and abundance of the age—set the tone for all public buildings. The expanded Carnegie Institute, one of the largest and most stately cultural palaces of its time in America, might be said to sum up the progressive social ideals as well as the architectural practice of the nineteenth century.

Two years after the original building was dedicated, it became evident that it was too small, and Andrew Carnegie on one of his visits to Pittsburgh suggested that plans be made for its enlargement. In April, 1899, he offered the Board of Trustees $1,750,000 to initiate the work, but changes in the plans of Alden and Harlow (who had been commissioned to design the new work) had augmented the estimated cost to $3,600,000.

Their studies (a preliminary version of the executed work) were shown at the Pittsburgh Architectural Club exhibition of 1900, and it was apparently this group of drawings that was approved by Carnegie in April of 1901. However, W. N. Frew of the Board of Trustees at the same time submitted for Mr. Carnegie's examination plans for an even larger project. When told that the latest proposed structure would cost $5,000,000, Mr. Carnegie replied, as if he were purchasing some small object, that "by all means we should have these plans," and forthwith wrote a note to his financial agent in Pittsburgh instructing him to place that sum to the credit of the Board.

Later, even Andrew Carnegie could not comprehend that this palace—all marbled and golden—had arisen by his agency, and in his dedicatory speech of 1907 he said, in effect, that he could not quite believe in its reality, that it seemed almost like something encountered in a dream.

FIRST FLOOR

1. President's Office
2. Carnegie Institute
   Society
   CARNEGIE MAGAZINE
3. Art and Nature Shop
4. Buildings Office
5. Museum Office
6. Education Office
7. Checkroom
   Post Office
   Lost and Found
8. Deadline for Wildlife
9. Decorative Arts Hall
10. Miniature Rooms
11. Hall of Architecture
12. Music Hall
13. Music Hall Foyer
14. Insects and
    Invertebrates
15. Marine Hall
16. Paleozoic Hall
17. Dinosaur Hall
18. Fossil Mammals
19. Birds and Reptiles
20. Viking Hall
21. Tri-State Room
22. Lecture Hall
    The Library
23. Library Office
24. Charging Booth
25-29. Lending Division
30. Boys and Girls Room
31. Library Personnel Office
32. Financial Offices

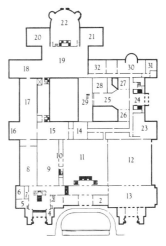

SECOND FLOOR

1. Museum of Art Office
2. Education Offices
3. Treasure Room
4. Music Hall, first balcony
5. Heads and Horns
6. Mammal Hall
7. Boone and Crockett
   Club
8. Botany Hall
   The Library
9. General Reference
10. Music Division
11. Pennsylvania Room
12. Art Division (*Library*)
13. Stacks
14. Periodical Room
15. Microfilm Room
A. Old Master and
   American Paintings
B. Modern European
   Paintings
C. Contemporary Art
D. Prints and Drawings
E-H Art Exhibition Galleries

THIRD FLOOR

1. Music Hall, second
   balcony
2. Hobby Hall
3. Transportation
4. American Indians
   and Eskimos
5. Ancient Near East
   The Library
6. Science and
   Technology Department
7. Stacks
I-R Art Exhibition Galleries

One of the frescoed printer's marks in the Reference Room of Carnegie Library, 1895

Michelangelo by J. Massey Rhind

Henry Moore "Reclining Figure" recently placed before the carriage entrance

12

Carriage entrance, 1908

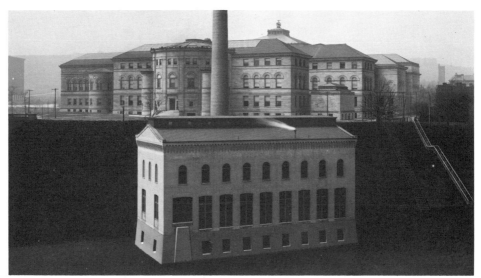

View of Carnegie Institute from Junction Hollow in 1907 showing power plant

Engine Room, 1908

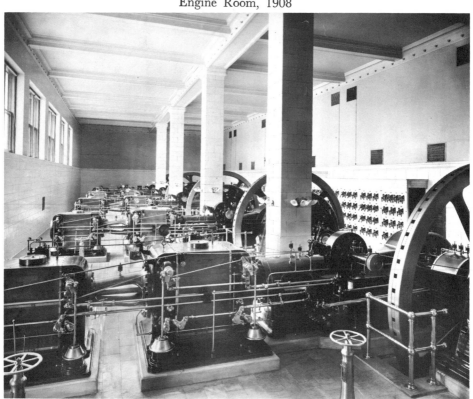

14

Ladies Salon off the balcony of the Music Hall Foyer, 1908, now headquarters for the Women's Committee of the Museum of Art.

Interior of Music Hall looking toward procenium, 1895

Auditorium of Music Hall, 1895

Slowly the great building began to materialize after the donor had given his approval. The enlarged scale of the structure had necessitated the acquisition of more land, and excavation was not begun until November, 1903; in July, 1904, the contract for the superstructure was awarded to William Miller and Son. The final plans and drawings were completed by Alden and Harlow in the spring of 1904. (All the drawings—some two thousand of them—for both the first and second Carnegie buildings, purchased from the architects in the 1930's, are now in the care of the building manager at the Institute.)

It is possible that much of the design of the new addition was the work of Howard K. Jones (1873-1931), who was chief draftsman for Alden and Harlow at the time of the construction although he later became a partner. Richard Hooker and John Henry Craner, who were also in the office at this period, were mentioned by Mr. Craner himself, shortly before his death, as contributors to the design.

The Institute was certainly the largest commission that ever came to the firm, and it must have required considerable cooperation from all members of the staff. The construction proceeded without any undue delay, and the structure was dedicated by Andrew Carnegie on April 11, 1907, as the climax of three days of impressive ceremonies.

The sheer size of the structure constitutes its first claim to the beholder's attention. The corridor mileage of the Pentagon or the frontages of the Escorial arouse astonishment or excite wonder quite apart from the merits or shortcomings of the buildings of which they form a part, and Carnegie Institute in its magnitude forms only a little smaller unit in this colossal company. Its dimensions are undeniably impressive. This huge, uneven mass, roughly square in shape except for the projecting lecture hall wing in the rear, consists of a complex of rooms, halls, and courts that covers nearly five acres of ground. There are almost twenty acres of floor space in the building, which has a frontage of 460 feet on Forbes Avenue and 640 feet on the Schenley Park Plaza side, and it is 138 feet high from the basement to the top of the dome. The three-story arrangement has been continued from the first version, so that the facades are uniform in dimension all around the building. The statistics on the masonry seem almost mountainous; 165,000 square feet of cut stone were used on the exterior and 6,000 tons of marble on the interior.

Stylistically, the building displays a further mutation of the Classical revival of the late-nineteenth century; the French manner of the École des Beaux-Arts was, in large degree, substituted for the Italianate mode—the latter so well exemplified in the first Carnegie building. The neo-Baroque massing seen in embryo in the first Music Hall treatment grew and triumphed completely in the great domed mass of the new work, and it is, as it were, a culmination of the revived

Classical manner, an ornate, imperial gigantism that reflected the magnificence and the *brio* of the beginning century.

In the French neo-Baroque manner of the Beaux-Arts, subdued though it was, Alden and Harlow were using Parisian architectural argot that had become an international idiom and that was already extensively fashionable in America. Not only in this city but throughout the Western world, all types of buildings in the neo-Baroque style were rising as evidences of the glittering power of the new age.

The change from the smaller, provincial elegance of the first building to the Edwardian grandeur of the second can be traced in the surviving drawings. The form of the final version—including the square dome, the two pavilions of the main façade, and the general layout—was already well developed in the exhibited sketches of 1900. Although the quattrocento detailing of the Library façade had been re-used on the projected Forbes Avenue front, the pavilions were quite different in treatment, and the plan shows many divergencies from that of the executed work. The 1900 scheme, with its inconclusive grandeur and too contrived effects, has the air of a Beaux-Arts *esquisse,* the remote, studied intricacy of purely paper architecture.

An enlargement, a simplification, and a refinement of the main elements of the 1900 composition are visible in the final drawings of 1904. The note of quietude and sobriety so consonant with the general tone of Pittsburgh architecture is a result here of the reduction of the Beaux-Arts theme to its simplest terms. Some of the Italianate features in the interest of uniformity have been retained on the new walls, and the Florentine mullioned windows of both 1891 and 1900 have here become plain arched openings which, however, do echo Alberti's wall arcades of the Tempio Malatestiano (begun 1446) at Rimini. These had been first adapted by Labrouste in his Bibliothèque Ste. Geneviève (1843-50) at Paris and notably again in the Boston Library. The Bostonian doorways with their scrolled keystones first used on the 1891 Library façade appeared again on the new Forbes Avenue entrances. But the Italian reminiscences evident in the general ensemble remain a muted accompaniment to the major French theme.

It is the projecting pavilions of the main front with their dramatic Corinthian loggias that assert so definitely the Parisian note and preserve so elegantly the ebullient 1900 air even into our own time. The heavy bilateral symmetry of the whole façade is an echo of that of the Paris Opéra and the Library of Congress at Washington, although the general treatment of the mass and the detailing are quite different. The massing of the roofs is French. A new roof of green alodine aluminum in emulation of the old copper sheathing was completed in 1957.

18 The enormous central dome that presides so formidably like an

enthroned dowager over the rest of the building is essentially Baroque in its compositional function, but also reflects in its ancestry the nineteenth-century interest in archaeology. The square dome was fairly common in the late-nineteenth century, but it may not be too fanciful to assume that the broad, flattened pyramid of the Carnegie dome was only another version, very freely adapted, of the Halicarnassian motif—or at least of the pyramidal roof assigned to the Mausoleum by the restorers.

There is in the general composition, as Montgomery Schuyler noted in 1911, a certain separation between the mass of the new work and the older Library section, but this is only apparent—and not to a really troubling degree — on the Park Plaza side of the building, since the dome almost succeeds in tying in the disparate elements of the scheme. Schuyler also praised the bronze statuary of the Forbes Avenue pavilions, which adorns and accents, precisely and scrupulously, the Beaux-Arts theme. This is definitely architectural sculpture of the Classical type, very ably executed by John Massey Rhind (1858?-1936), who, like Andrew Carnegie, had been born in Scotland. His work is competent if not very exciting. Groups representing literature, music, science, and art are placed atop the corner piers of the pavilions, and figures of Bach, Galileo, Shakespeare, and Michelangelo preside on either side of the two lateral entrances. These lofty and pensive spirits, frozen in the calm repose of bronze, form the proper guardians and sentinels of our cultural palace.

The architects in planning the new work had, again, to take into consideration the already existing building, and although there are some faults in the layout, they did for the most part a very creditable job. As evidence of the esteem in which their work was held at the time, the ground-floor plan was illustrated in the eleventh edition of the *Encyclopaedia Britannica* (1910-11) as representative of the modern American museum on a large scale.

Some attempt was made to maintain axial relationships in the museum and art-gallery sections, but the general effect of the placing of the grand halls with their subsidiary rooms would scarcely conform to the strictest tenets of classical planning, and perhaps this very lack of rigidity has a sort of haphazard charm lacking in more straitly ordered compositions. The notable lack of the extended vista (at least in the case of the great "show" rooms) is here abundantly compensated for by oblique and angular glimpses of brief truncated distances and sudden corners. Generally speaking, the exhibition galleries of the Museum are concentrated at the back of the structure, those devoted to the Fine Arts are in front.

The original building was taken over completely by the Library   19 after some remodeling that included the handsome staircase of Tennessee marble, whose neo-Classical austerity is relieved by seventeenth-century molded and painted ceilings. The most important addition to the Library was the great eleven-story stack built at the rear of the old storage wing; constructed of glass, steel, and terra cotta, it is the most modern looking part of the structure.

In terms of construction methods, the first version of the Institute represents a transitional phase between the old masonic tradition and the new architecture based on the steel frame—steel beams were used in the old structure merely to support the walls and the roof. The new work of 1904-07 is much more modern since the steel framework is the real core of the structure.

There are several large architecturally treated rooms in the new work, and of these the grandest and most spectacular is undoubtedly the Foyer of the Music Hall, which is one of the most splendid examples of Edwardian display in America, concerning which, more later.

Another is the great staircase hall at the opposite end of the building that gives access to the art galleries. Here the wide burnished expanses of Eschallion and Hauteville marble rising through three stories, the opulently patterned floor, and the swirling tenuosities of the murals set eminently the tone of the building, proclaim its subdued palatial richness, though the pride of the ascending flights is not royal, but municipal. The idea of *escaliers d'honneur* such as this is assentially Baroque, and the prototype of our stairway is undoubtly that of the Paris Opéra, but the sinuous feminine pomp of Paris has been metamorphosed into a quiet, angular masculinity. Pittsburgh is an intensely masculine city and so is much of its architecture, and nowhere is that virility shown more straitly than in this stair hall.

The colonnade of the first floor exhibits a severe application of the Doric motif of late-eighteenth-century neo-Classicism. Above, however, the style changes, and the Corinthian gallery of the second floor has a monumental cinquecento nobility in keeping with the Italianate detail of the exterior. The metal grilles of the balustrades and the bronze elevator doors with their pleasant Beaux-Arts ornament palliate a little the marble rigors. All this muscular *brio*, this spare, mannered magnificance, is quite in contrast with the Edwardian ornateness of the Foyer.

The stair hall murals representing The Crowning of Labor by John White Alexander (1856-1915), the Pittsburgh artist, provide a softly feminine foil to the pervasive austerity of the architecture. They play a supporting role, advance a subsidiary cause, and they do it adequately if not triumphantly. The painter's platitudinous forms and floating pallors have the charming quality of good Edwardian magazine

20

illustration, and as such they not inappropriately footnote this massive display of early-twentieth-century architectural rhetoric. The stair hall itself illustrates and defines the spirit of Pittsburgh much better than the paintings.

The Hall of Architecture and the Sculpture Court are also of great interest and are taken up in later chapters. Two other rooms, one on each side of the main automobile entrance—the Founder's Room and the President's Office—have a large Edwardian richness, both of material, and in the case of the former, of ornament. The polyglot Eclectic tongue is again in evidence in the Founder's Room, where the French sixteenth-century beamed and painted ceiling and the early-nineteenth-century Classical paneling consort well with the quattrocento fireplace of carved Istrian marble and the modern plate-glass windows. In the plenitude of its red mahogany, its severe Red Numidian marble fireplace, and the sombre green of its walls, the President's office echoes the luxurious austerity of the great stair hall, and it is—like something out of a novel by Edith Wharton—very eminently the early-twentieth-century office of a business executive.

In the Carnegie Institute the great rooms, with their freight and plunder of the past, seem to float, as it were, above a multitude of workshops and laboratories; they are upraised, supported, and maintained by a marvelously active little city that is essential to the structure's very existence.

One of these rooms in the basement—the engine room—possesses a compelling interest, a magnificence, quite equal to that of any of the great galleries above. At present it contains four generators, powered by steam from the Bellefield Boiler Plant, that manufacture electricity for the building. It is thoroughly utilitarian, but highly ornamental— only an Edwardian architect would have ventured to provide a place of such elegance to house machinery. With its marble floor, its white terra-cotta walls, and its instrument panels of marble and brass, it seems almost like a ballroom for machines, where the intricate, precise movements of the generators constitute a sort of perpetual mechanical ballet.

A long corridor-tunnel conducts the great steam pipes from the boiler plant, located in the ravine below the Institute, into the basement of the building. The plant with its severe grey brick flanks and Italian medieval corbeling was designed as an integral part of the structure in 1904, but in 1943 it was enlarged so that it might serve other buildings in Oakland. A modern concrete chimney stack, 255 feet high, has been constructed next to the slightly smaller original stack.

Foyer of the Music Hall, 1907

II

THE TRIUMPHANT STONE:

The Foyer of Carnegie Music Hall

ON THE MORNING of April 11, 1907, there gathered at a municipal reception in the Foyer of Carnegie Institute a large assembly of important personages—diplomatic, academic, professional, and financial—to celebrate the dedication of the new building that was a gift from Andrew Carnegie to the City of Pittsburgh.

The brilliance of the company was in a way outshone by the splendors of the Foyer itself. Possibly these notables should have moved about to the music of Elgar, but the music would not have been needed since the architecture is such a perfect embodiment of Edwardian self-satisfaction and sumptuous display. And even today the glamor and the glory, although a little dimmed and tarnished, have not departed. These fanfares of marble and pyrotechnical exhibitions of gilded plaster are as remarkable to behold now as they were then. The Foyer is certainly the most splendid ceremonial hall in America (where halls of ceremony are not numerous), and probably it can hold its own with most European examples of the type—if not on the score of taste, at least on that of richness and bravura.

There is no doubt that the Foyer was amply conceived, even by the standards of an ample age, and very richly executed, at a time when richness was considered a *sine qua non* of the architecture of public buildings. The mere recital of its physical dimensions is impressive: the room extends the entire width of the Music Hall and is 60 feet wide, 135 feet long, and 45 feet high. A great colonnade of twenty-four marble columns, 28 feet high, supports, at the level of the Music Hall gallery, a balcony that entirely circles the room. The columns bear Corinthian capitals in gold, and they are surmounted by a lavishly decorated cornice and ceiling.

French in style—of that neo-Baroque type which had so dominated the Parisian École des Beaux-Arts during the late nineteenth and early twentieth centuries — the Foyer quite lacks the movement and exuberance of Garnier's Paris Opera House (1863-75) and the buildings of the Paris Expositions of 1889 and 1900; it is more nearly akin, in a certain coolness and soberness of tone, to French Classical work of the seventeenth and eighteenth centuries. In its lavish use of luxurious materials and the heavy elegance of its detailing, the Foyer is a true and representative monument of the Edwardian era—that period between 1900 and 1914 — the high summer and heyday of the capitalist world.

It was that world which constructed this brilliant hall as a place of promenade and a visible embodiment in marble and gold of its pride and its power, its industrial and financial achievements, its weighty and polished richness, and its luxurious if rather self-conscious devotion to culture. The Foyer is a monument, not to the pomp of princes and the circumstances of kings but to the majesty and affluence of merchants and manufacturers—that class which had risen to power during the nineteenth century and now wished to show forth its strength in a tangible way. The social emphasis had shifted from the royal and the aristocratic to the bourgeois and municipal, and the art of building reflected the change.

Sumptuosity was not, however, eschewed by the new patrons, and the public buildings of the Edwardians were compact of ceremony and display; they seem to be always, in retrospect, *en grande tenue,* as it were. The dress for the occasion was intended to be magnificent. If the style was borrowed from the past, it didn't much matter; the cloth was cut to suit the spirit of the new age, and the garment was worn with a certain air of assurance. The architecture of the Foyer reflects the tempered and restrained Baroque of the age of Louis XIV, but no one would mistake it for a work of the seventeenth century; in its general tone and feeling, as well as in some of its detail, it is purely a room of the early twentieth century.

The two flanking pavilions of the main façade, with their Parisian elegance and grace, announce most persuasively on the exterior the Edwardian grandeur of the Foyer. One of these pavilions, with its sculptured representations of Literature and Music atop the corner piers, gives access, through chastely designed bronze portals, to the Foyer. We are prepared for the coming marmoreal wonders by two vestibules lined with orange-colored dark Montarenti Sienna marble, overarched by gilded ornamental ceilings. Even here, in this small place of entrance, everything glows and shines—the gold leaf, marble, and plate-glass doors—for one is, after all, entering the Edwardian world.

No social group since the Romans, it is probably safe to say, had such a passion for marble as the Edwardians. Indeed their admiration for all rich and glamorous stones—exemplified not only in architectural adornments but also in such minor objects as the luxurious and precious toys of Fabergé—assumed almost the proportions of a cult or, rather, it was only one evidence of the general cult of *grand luxe* so characteristic of the period. And the shining stone and the gold looked even richer when seen through heavy polished sheets of plate glass. Here in the Foyer vestibules, however, the display of glass is unostentatious, merely a small sumptuous note that serves to give a preparatory glimpse of the glories beyond.

It does not matter whether one sees the Foyer for the first or the hundredth time, the first impression is apt to be rather overwhelming. There is something at once exhilarating and oppressive in this plenitude of marble—the richly patterned red Castelpoggia, white Italian, and Vert Antique floor, the dark polished rotundity of the columns (the pillars at the angles of the room are, however, square), and the rich but delicate colors of the inlaid walls. In one's everyday utilitarian clothing one feels strangely out of place here— all the marble and gold cry out for the complementary shimmer of silk and satin. Such architectural formality seems to demand ceremonies that even the opulent Edwardian era could not provide, and the great hall is redolent of its aristocratic ancestry.

The ceremonial hall has a long tradition in Western architectural history, where the gallery, with or without columns, was important as a place of meeting, procession, or promenade. The immediate prototype of the Carnegie gallery is certainly the Foyer of the Paris Opéra; the latter is similar to the Pittsburgh room in spirit if not in execution, as the decorative schemes are rather different— at Paris, for instance, the colonnades are lacking. The lush, Second-Empire over-elaboration of the Opéra Foyer with its almost frightening wealth of adornment is in subtle contrast to our room where the subdued richness of ornament bears witness to the fact that, if Pittsburghers did not take their architectural pleasures sadly, they at least took them with quietness and decorum.

It cannot be contended that the logical and finely articulated plan of the Paris Opéra was emulated to any extent at Pittsburgh, although it must be admitted that the architects did the best they could in fitting the new addition to an already existing building. It is possible that the design of the new structure, as well as the Foyer itself, was for the most part the work of Howard K. Jones, the chief draftsman in the office of Alden and Harlow. Whether or not he was also the most important designer, he must have had, by virtue of his position, a great deal to do with the execution of the design.

The progression of rooms from the first vestibule of the Foyer to the Music Hall itself is logical and coherent. It is unfortunate, however, that the stairways are so indifferently treated and that the carriage entrance should have been placed at such a distance from the Music Hall. If the treatment of the stairways is dull, the quiet decorative scheme of the connecting room between the Foyer and the Hall, with its paneling of light Montarenti Sienna marble and its gilded vaulting, provides an unobtrusive connecting link between the French opulence of the one and the quattrocento delicacy of the other.

It is certainly the abundance of marble in the Foyer that provides   25 most eminently the expansive Edwardian tone. The index to the marbles, preserved among the Foyer drawings, has almost the effect of an elaborate French menu of the period. Eschallion, Istrian, Vert Tinos, Hauteville, Red Numidian, and Montarenti Sienna sound good enough to eat, and it is most appropriate that the Foyer has been used as a dining hall on occasion. The great Vert Tinos columns—they are all constructed in three segments with separate bases—were shaped in the marble contractor's yards and then put in place. The Eschallion wall panels, which are separated by pilasters of Vert Tinos, are intricately inlaid with varicolored marbles, and these designs were executed by special workmen on the spot. Over the doorways are handsomely carved cartouches of unpolished marble, which provide welcome accents of relief among so many shining surfaces.

At one end of the room is a wide recess, screened by four smaller monolithic Tinos columns, that contains the bronze statue of Andrew Carnegie. At the other extremity of the hall, unpolished carved piers uphold the hooded fireplace, which bears the arms of the City of Pittsburgh in the center of the hood. This mantel provides another stylistic and rather anachronistic note in the design of the Foyer, since it is a quattrocento echo from the earlier building.

All this glowing splendor suggests the rich snobbism, the hectic éclat, of the hotels de luxe of the period and recalls forcibly the heavy grandeur of Edwardian banking rooms.

Wilmer M. Jacoby, whose father, as proprietor of a marble yard in Philadelphia, did some work on the decoration of the Foyer, was very helpful in supplying the writer with information on this aspect of the construction of the building. The marble contract was in the hands of the general contractor for the structure, William F. Miller and Sons, a local firm who had undertaken some important jobs in Pittsburgh including the Frick Building (1902). Since the Carnegie contract was probably the largest marble job undertaken in the county prior to 1904, there was no one company in America equipped to handle it, and the work was parceled out among several companies in Philadelphia, Baltimore, Chicago, and Buffalo. One B. P. Young in the employ of Miller, acted as coordinator of their activities, and he was sent to Greece to arrange for the shipments of the Vert Tinos for the Foyer as well as Pentelic marble for Sculpture Court.

If the unfluted marble columns suggest late-eighteenth-century neo-Classicism, and the balcony railings have a Louis Seize quality, the golden ceiling is entirely Baroque in feeling. All of it is molded plaster covered with gold leaf. The Corinthian capitals, also of gilded plaster, are handsome and properly in scale, but the entablature above them is perhaps a little overfussy, plagued as it is by the usual garlands and cartouches. In the triangular indentations of the coved part of the ceiling — an echo of those in the Music Hall — are lunettes containing larger, freestanding cartouches and more garlands — standard devices of the neo-Baroque designer. The great ropelike bands of fruit and leaves outlining the indentations of the cove and the outer compartments of the central coffered ceiling recall most strongly the seventeenth century.

It is interesting that the architects did not use the painted panel— a favorite motif of Baroque ceiling designers—in the overall design, and those sections of the roof not gilded were tinted a pale grey. As one looks up at it from the main floor, the ceiling seems to open outward like some fabulous flower. These intricate recessional concavities, these remote dim glowings and corruscations, golden depths on further depths of richness, at once enchant and soothe the wondering eye. There is little Baroque in Pittsburgh, and it has never been really at home here, but in this one monument, at least, it abides supremely in our midst.

The elaborate concavity of the main ceiling is echoed in the gilded barrel vaults of the balcony corridors, but the groined vaults at the four angles of the room are extremely weak. The wall cornice below this vaulting has a series of molded brackets bearing the names of famous composers that recalls the frieze of names on the outer cornice of the building. This lettered compendium of musical fame in the balcony constitutes a rather self-conscious Edwardian cultural note, as well as a dictionary of those musicians who were in favor during the early twentieth century.

A small consideration of the history of the construction of the ceiling furnishes us with some interesting social and artistic glimpses of the period. A. Russell Robinson, now deceased, who came to Pittsburgh from Philadelphia in 1905 as superintendent for the plaster work in the building, especially the Foyer, was also good enough to provide the writer with considerable information. Ornamental plaster work was, in those days, a branch of the art of sculpture, and workers in the field had to be highly skilled. All the details of the ceiling were molded and cast in a studio set up in the building, then put in place by the craftsmen. The superintendent had eighty-five plasterers working under him; the most important of them were the model-makers, the modelers, and the casters—the latter group mostly Italians. The foreman of the model-makers (those who made the molds) was a temperamental Frenchman who had been educated at the Ecole des Beaux-Arts, and the foreman of the modelers was also French. Howard Jones, who represented the architects, looked in on the work occasionally. In general the plasterers received $4.20 a day for a forty-four hour week. All in all, the Foyer ceiling cost approximately $14,000.00 when it was completed; one hesitates to think what it would cost today, even if the craftsmen could be found who could execute it or a patron desirous of it.

From the central rosettes of the coffered ceiling are suspended four golden chandeliers, interesting in that they were not intended to emulate Renaissance candle fixtures, but were designed as objects for the diffusion of electric light. Designing of electrical fixtures—still a relatively new field—challenged the ingenuity of the Edwardians, and the neo-Baroque designers had considerable scope to display originality and inventiveness. Aldous Huxley has remarked somewhere that what the Baroque needed was electricity; the neo-Baroque had it in abundance—the lighting effects aimed at by the Edwardians were, however, not subtle and artfully dramatic as in modern buildings, but forthright and even a little crude.

In the Foyer, naked light bulbs provided the illumination, and there was no attempt to conceal them on the chandeliers; a handsome scaffolding was prepared in which they could abundantly shine. The Music Hall itself has a coronet of light bulbs across the proscenium arch. In those days, there could not be enough electricity. The official description of the dedicatory reception in the Foyer says that the hall was illuminated by "a thousand electric lights," and there are almost unreserved pride and triumph in that statement.

There are two minor rooms in connection with the Foyer that have a certain interest, although they have both lost their original functions. The first of these is the large "ladies' salon" off the balcony, facing toward the loggia at the front of the building. Although elegantly designed in an extremely subdued Garnieresque manner and painted in a pale green-grey picked out in gold, it has the faint chilliness of a railway-station waiting room. It was probably intended simply as a meeting place for ladies during an Edwardian intermission (before 1914 respectable Pittsburgh women did not smoke in public), and, with its original deep-red velvet furniture providing a background for the elaborate toilettes of the time, it must have been a handsome spectacle. Today all but one of its grey marble archways have been filled in. The room is now being used by the Women's Committee of the Museum of Art, perhaps a logical modern development. There was also a smoking room for men in the basement, which, with piers encased in Red Numidian marble and a vaguely Elizabethan ceiling, provided a properly masculine atmosphere for entr'acte cigars. It is now a classroom for the hobby painting classes.

It was a happy thought that prompted the resurrection from storage of many of the Museum's late-Victorian and Edwardian paintings and their placement on the walls of the Foyer and the stair halls. Their golden frames and glossy painted surfaces, as well as their subject matter, contribute notably to the period tone of the room.

28

III

THE TOMB, THE TEMPLE, AND THE CASTS
The Hall of Architecture and Sculpture Court

ARCHAEOLOGY, THE STUDY of human life of the past and its monuments, developed very rapidly as a science in the nineteenth century, and exerted a profound influence on the architecture of the Eclectic period. The all-pervasive influence of the new science may be seen at Carnegie Institute, where the building is no less a product of archaeological research than the collections it encloses. The Hall of Architecture, Sculpture Court, and their groups of plaster casts, still so notably intact, illustrate not only the architectural tone of the Edwardian age, but also museum practice of the time. Here in these halls one may confront the varied faces of history as well as the masks those faces may present to the modern eye.

That angular glass bell, the great square dome of the Institute, itself a memorial of the Mausoleum of Halicarnassus, preserves in its depths, as in a tomb chamber, possibly the largest group of architectural casts still on exhibition in America. These are the reproduced plaster bones of Western building history. Less lofty, but more richly decorated, inasmuch as it was adapted from the habitation of a goddess, Sculpture Court, a marble reminiscence of the Parthenon, was constructed next the Mausoleum as if to remind us of the mansions beyond mortality. This marmoreal hall, reduced from divinity in its Pittsburgh version, does not know Athena in ivory and gold as did the Parthenon, but only a minor assembly, a plaster Olympus of classical sculptural moulages. Despite their dependence on archaeological themes, however, the two great rooms are definitely architectural documents of their day of origin; in their skylit amplitude, their aspiring bright enclosure of space, they are resplendent examples of Edwardian expansiveness and display.

Before we consider the cast architecture of Carnegie's Hall, we must consider the structure of the room itself. In our plaster symphony, the archaeological theme is introduced at the beginning—*forte* and *con brio*. The published accounts of the labors of a Schliemann or a Layard engaged the popular as well as the architectural eye, and the discoveries of the archaeologists added more material to the great midden heap of the past in which the architect, as well as the public for whom he built, searched for constructional novelties. One of these "buried" buildings was the great Halicarnassian tomb built in 353 b. c., as a memorial to the Asian king Mausolus. In ancient times one of the Seven Wonders

29

of the World, it had fallen into ruin, but its remains were excavated by Sir Charles Newton in 1856. From the resurrected stones and carvings, nineteenth-century architects attempted, with the help of Classical literary descriptions, to make restorations on paper, and from thence it was only a step to adapting the form of the structure for contemporary uses. Alden and Harlow, the architects of Carnegie Institute, used the theme as a point of departure for the design of the Hall of Architecture.

The great hall beneath the Halicarnassian dome is a huge, uneven cube of truly Baroque dimensions—it is 125 feet long, 126 feet wide, and a little more than 76 feet high. This, the main-axial room of the whole Institute complex, is quite forlorn of marble and glory, and its bland plaster banality is rather disappointing inasmuch as one might have expected in this place the most dazzling display of interior magnificence. Here, under the coved Baroque ceiling with its great skylight, the palatial note lingers thinly and without emphasis.

A further and very interesting reminiscence of the Mausoleum is to be found in the colonnade of twenty-eight Ionic columns that surrounds the room and carries a gaunt balcony with a glass floor; these pillars are an adaptation of the tomb's external peristyle turned inward, as it were, a curious transposition of decorative elements that we may notice again in the frieze of Sculpture Court. This shifting and interpenetration of exterior and interior parts, this free use of stylistic motives plucked from the ruins of the past, suggest the mobility of stage scenery—sets that could be moved about to create any effect the Eclectic architect wished. The general effect of the Hall of Architecture is quiet and subdued; haunted by its abounding plaster ghosts, it is flooded from above by a luminous hazy radiance—so appropriate to a resurrected tomb.

The gaunt and rather bare art museums erected in the New World during the late nineteenth and early twentieth centuries lacked, in many cases, any extensive collections of original material, and administrators were constrained to fill their galleries with reproductions. The case of Carnegie Institute was certainly no exception to this state of affairs. Something had to be placed in the galleries of the great new building opened in 1907, and since no large supply of actual works of art was available, a collection of reproductions took their place. Casts of sculpture had already become a part of the collections even before the structure was enlarged, but the rebuilding was looked upon as an opportunity to augment the group of moulages and to set up displays comparable to those of the museums of Boston, New York, and Chicago. As early as 1903, John Beatty, the director of the Department of Fine Arts, was engaged in choosing plaster examples of architecture and sculpture to fill the projected Hall of Architecture and Sculpture Court. There were commercial establishments in the chief European countries whose business it was to supply such items, and many of the minor objects at the Institute were ordered from their catalogues. Some French museums like the Louvre and the Trocadéro had studios of their own where casts could be made to order from existing molds, but some of the largest moulages in the Hall of Architecture, such as that of the façade of the twelfth-century French Romanesque church of St. Gilles du Gard, had to be specially commissioned. Concerning the moulages, extensive correspondence from the year 1905-06 still exists in the files of the Museum of Art at the Institute, and it may be interesting to give some small account of the St. Gilles cast as an essay in a neglected facet of past museology.

Cast of the St. Gilles portal in the Hall of Architecture, 1908

One of the largest architectural casts ever made (it is 75 feet long and 38 feet high), the façade is easily the dominant element in the Hall of Architecture, and it effectively hides Mausolus' colonnade on the side facing the entrance. No molds for it were in existence, and special permission had to be obtained from the French government to have the portal of the Priory Church molded. These molds were   31 plaster or gelatin impressions taken directly from the structure, from which the casts themselves were made. The work was executed by a group of workmen under the direction of the chief of the cast studio at the Trocadéro, and the contract price was 40,000 francs, or about $8,000.00 at the then current rate of exchange — although a separate and unspecified donation had to be made to the municipality of St. Gilles for the use of its façade, and freight transportation had to be paid.

As the casts were made from the molds, they were packed in crates and dispatched to America from Marseilles, the nearest port. The task of making the reproductions was completed at St. Gilles in the summer of 1906, but the many sections still had to be assembled on this side of the Atlantic. It is interesting to note that this plaster transplantation of a complete European façade preceded the transfer of actual buildings to this country. (One American millionaire at a slightly later period bought a whole monastery and had it shipped home.)

The plans of the cast were sent by registered mail to America, and a French workman, M. Boucholtz, was dispatched to Pittsburgh, where he was to assist in the erection of the façade under the direction of John Beatty's assistant, August Teller. A special framework of timber and wire was constructed, on which the cast sections were carefully mounted and joined so to give the impression of a coherent monolithic whole. It has been said that the brownish coloring was added to the cast (possibly in emulation of the fashionable American brownstone) by one of the workmen; this at least redeemed the structure from the ghostly pallor peculiar to casts even if it may not be physically accurate. Finished in time for the opening of the new Institute building in April, 1907, this reproduced fragment of the medieval past in all its intricate Romanesque majesty provided one of the most spectacular sights of the grand occasion.

It is still one of the most interesting and dramatic objects in the Institute collections. Like some fabulous and forsaken city in a medieval tapestry, it hovers hauntingly under Mausolus' dome, inhabited by silent, fantastic beasts and broken Roman columns, by frozen saints and fairy-tale foliage. However engaging as stage scenery, this plaster replica cannot, in the end, be considered a valid historical document; it is an illusion, a mask, behind which we may discern dimly the real face of the past. But even if it is a mask of the past, it does strike the note of grace in the harsh industrial climate of Pittsburgh; it emphasizes an achieved state of artistic grandeur, albeit at one remove.

The question of illusionism becomes more complicated when we consider another cast—the section of the "order" (comprising a column and part of the entablature) of the Mausoleum at Halicarnassus erected

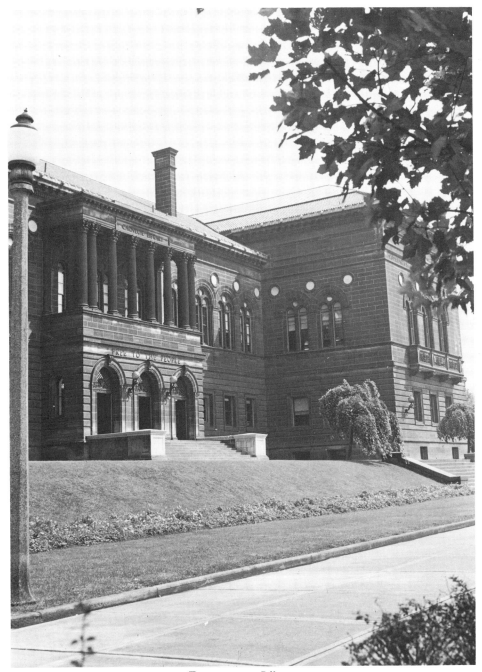

Entrance to Library

View of Main Reference Room, 1908

Lending department of Library as it looks today

Staircase of Library, 1908

The library in use through the years

The library in use through the years

Library stack building, 1908

Hall of Architecture collections are used as models for young artists

Scaife Collection of Miniatures

Lecture Hall as it looks today

Grand staircase with the Alexander murals

against the Hall of Architecture's Ionic colonnade, itself an adaptation of the columniation of the Asian tomb. The original of the "order" cast, now in the British Museum, is in itself a restoration reconstructed from fragments found during Newton's excavations; it displays a coarser, more vigorous use of the Ionic moif than the Hall colonnade, which favors the subdued grace of the Erechtheum columns on the Acropolis.

Behind the storied face of St. Gilles, among the phantoms of Gothic capitals and Renaissance balconies, is displayed, most appropriately, a group of Neapolitan statuary, pots, and furniture, facsimiles of those dug from the ruins of Pompeii and Herculaneum, destroyed by the eruption of Vesuvius in A.D. 79. These heterogeneous objects, memorials of Roman domestic life, are part of some three hundred reproductions of bronzes in the Naples Museum and were given to the Department of Fine Arts by Andrew Carnegie in 1901. A variation on the theme of the reproduced artifact, these admirable imitations with their patination and marks of time and age are as like the originals as art and skill could make them. Other American museums possess similar objects ordered, as was the Carnegie group, from the catalogues of Sabatino de Angelis & Son (for the Italians were particularly good at this type of craftsmanship). In the hands of these Italian artisans, the art of reproduction comes perilously close to that of forgery (one might say that the difference here between the two is merely one of intention), for the Carnegie replicas come about as close to the real thing as you can get. These bronze articles, black or blue-green in color, form a series of brilliantly executed grace notes in the Hall of Architecture's plaster symphony.

One may note that the casts of the Hall of Architecture form a collection of examples from which the Eclectic architects borrowed, and there is no small resemblance between the plaster constructions in the Hall and the brick and stone buildings of the Oakland Civic Center just outside its walls.

Pittsburgh is probably fortunate in having preserved its casts *in situ,* this side of storage or the junk yard; the tide of fashion, notoriously wayward, may already be running in the direction of the Hall of Architecture, and who knows if pilgrims may not then come to visit our plaster paradise. There is really no end to the fascination of the place. Beyond its period quality and its practical purpose, its appeal to the modern sensibility is enormous—this great, jagged garden of dissimilar forms, these displaced ornamental fragments, the curious confrontations and juxtapositions, the looming gigantic portals that lead nowhere, and the specimen columns that support nothing compose the magnificent disordered landscape of a Mannerist or Surrealist dream. Pittsburghers, whatever may be their aesthetic reactions, have become used to the Hall 41 of Architecture, and they feel an affection for the place quite beyond any partiality for its artistic merits.

Over against the Hall of Architecture and connected with it by a small lobby that holds the Scaife Collection of Miniatures, lies Sculpture Court, another prime example of the Victorian and Edwardian passion for archaeological architecture. Neo-Classical, white and blandly luminous, it is, after the Music Hall Foyer, the richest and most elegant of the architecturally treated rooms at the Institute. Erected as an enclosed court for the display of casts of Classical sculpture, the blank pallors of the moulages complement dimly, although not incongruously, the glowing marble of the surrounding Doric and Ionic columns.

The Institute example is determinedly Greek although it has been "dressed up" with some Edwardian neo-Roman or even Renaissance elements, such as the pedestals and the scrolled metal balustrades on the balcony. It is probable that Alden and Harlow cribbed the idea of the room from Ernest Flagg's central atrium at the Corcoran Gallery of Art (1897) in Washington, D.C. The Pittsburgh architects, however, wished to speak even more forcibly the Grecian word, since the Carnegie court was built to resemble the cella of the Parthenon and constructed of Pentelic marble from the actual quarries that supplied the stone for that great Temple of Athena on the Acropolis.

A plaster reproduction of the Parthenon's Panathenaic frieze (given to the Institute by Andrew Carnegie in 1898) marches gravely around the room at the cornice line. It is placed at the approximate height from the cella floor of the Athenian original, but here it is on the inside of the building rather than the outside as at Athens. This constitutes another of those strange transpositions of exterior and interior architectural elements so agreeable to Eclectic architects.

Although modern attempts have been made to enliven the glowing general whiteness with seventeenth-century tapestries and Gothic furniture, the Court has a large grandeur, a chilly splendor that defies reduction to the status of a safe background for exhibited objects. Perhaps the plaster wraiths of Greece and Rome inhabit it with the least violence, the smallest incongruity. Of recent years exhibit cases housing objects of decorative art have been introduced but have also taken their place without disturbing the general tone.

Every age to some degree conceives the past in its own image, and Sculpture Court bears very noticeably the impress of the time it was built. Essentially a nineteenth-century dream of the Classical past carried over into the twentieth century, the Court rather plentifully exists in its own right, and the present-day critic has more or less to take it on its own terms.

Hall of Sculpture, 1907

Hall of the big bones, 1908

IV

THE URN AND THE TREE

A Commentary on the Early Days
of the Museum of Natural History

"TIME HATH ENDLESS RARITIES, and shows of all varieties; which reveals old things in heaven, makes new discoveries in earth, and even earth itself a discovery . . . and a large part of the earth is still in the Urne unto us."

With the advancement of science in the eighteenth and nineteenth centuries, Sir Thomas Browne's great "urne" became a cornucopia, spilling out across the continents a various store of objects — bones, knives, cities, and vanished forests. The surface of the world was also combed and swept; pictures, pots, flowers, machinery, and insects were gathered together, sorted, and classified. Storehouses were needed for all these displaced fragments of the past and present, and so the modern museum came about. These buildings, whether great or small, have become collectively a new urn, a simulacrum of the earth, though a repository separated, in most cases, from all mortuary significance. By no means are all museums fully alive or freed from the old urn, but a properly functioning museum is a vessel of life in our civilization. Among the latter is certainly Pittsburgh's Carnegie Museum, one of the leading natural history museums in the country. It is not alone an urn, since it may be looked upon as a storehouse that engenders life. The great court at the back of the building with its surrounding galleries illustrating the upward evolution of organic existence may symbolize a splendid tree with its roots in paleontology and its ultimate branches the life of Man and his activities. The reader or the visitor is hereby invited to inspect both the urn and the tree.

This particular tree had a rather difficult time gaining a root-hold in the industrial soil of Pittsburgh, for certainly the museum as an institution was late in coming to the city. The three exhibition rooms opened to the public at the first Carnegie Institute in 1895 were, however, an auspicious beginning and an augur of future growth. This embyro institution, new as it was to Pittsburgh, had behind it over a century of development in both Europe and America. Museums were, to some degree, an outgrowth of the Age of Enlightenment, and the Louvre, opened in Paris in 1793, was the forerunner and herald of a new type of public organization—the museum for the people.

There were embyro museums in America even by the eighteenth century. At Harvard College in 1750 and in Philadelphia before 1770, 45

Cabinets of Natural Curiosities were formed (possibly in emulation of the Ashmolean at Oxford, 1683), and at Charleston, South Carolina, a small natural history collection was opened in 1773, perhaps the first public museum in the United States. Collections gathered by private persons and shown to the public included those of P. E. du Simitière (opened to the public in 1782) and Charles Willson Peale (1785), both located in Philadelphia. Peale's museum contained the bones of a mastodon (unearthed in Connecticut in 1785), which the proprietor described as the "great American Incognitum." Rembrandt Peale, his son, also opened a museum in his house at Baltimore in 1814.

When one considers all the years during which Pittsburgh was museumless, it is highly interesting that the city did possess briefly a collection of the Peale type. The first museum organized west of the Allegheny Mountains, it was opened in a building at Fourth and Market Streets in 1828, and it was formed by the painter, James Reid Lambdin, who is chiefly remembered for his portraits. Lambdin was born in Pittsburgh in 1807, but he studied painting at Philadelphia, where he was undoubtedly familiar with Peale's repository. The Pittsburgh collection contained over fifty paintings (including canvases by Sully, West, Trumbull, and Lawrence), quadrupeds, minerals, fossils, coins, and Indian relics. This omnium-gatherum was, to some degree, supported by public subscription, but it suffered the same fate as its eastern forerunners; after four years it was closed, and Lambdin departed for Louisville, Kentucky, taking his collection with him. Essentially it was the old German princely *Wunderkammer*, democratized to cater at best to the tastes of a small provincial elite or at worst to the average gawker in the streets. It was, however, a museum, and during the early years of Pittsburgh's Iron Age the idea survived only in the library cabinets of part-time naturalists and the curio vitrines of Victorian matrons.

As the nineteenth century progressed, museums continued to be formed as part of the activities of historical societies, academies of science and art, and other cultural groups. In 1823-24 the first American museum building, Pilgrim Hall, was constructed at Plymouth, Massachusetts, in the Greek Revival style, which inaugurated in this country that long series of such structures in the Classical mode that was almost ubiquitous until quite recently. In 1869 the American Museum of Natural History was founded in New York, and it produced in the course of its development an institutional pattern that could be used by new institutions of similar nature.

After the first ardors of Pittsburgh's passion for manufacturing had somewhat abated, a renewed interest in the gentler aspects of life began once more to manifest itself. Cultural groups, including several

Museum of National History today

Museum of National History today

Soul Boat of Sesostris III

scientific organizations, were formed during the course of the nineteenth century, yet the mortality rate among them was high. The by-laws of an Academy of Science and Art chartered in 1860 contained the specifications for a small museum, but this venture never developed. Even as late as the 1880's, learned societies were not abundantly evident in the Gateway to the West, but those that did exist, such as the Engineers Society of Western Pennsylvania (formed in 1880), the Art Society (1873), and the Botanical Society of Western Pennsylvania (1886) were instrumental in forming another Academy of Science and Art that was incorporated in 1890. Such Pittsburgh collections as were deposited with the Academy after its foundation were first stored in the old Thaw mansion downtown until the new Museum could be built.

The first version of Carnegie Institute opened in 1895 was in reality Pittsburgh's first museum building. Within the new structure, however, the various museum functions were kept separate, and the art and natural history departments were firmly segregated in opposite wings, the latter occupying the southeast section. On the first floor there was a lecture hall, and on the second, three large exhibition galleries where was held the opening exhibition arranged by Gustav Guttenberg (d. 1896), the curator of the Academy of Science and Art. The Academy, which made its headquarters in the new building, turned its collections over to the Museum and in return was granted the privilege of using the lecture hall for its illustrated lecture series, still a prominent feature of its activities. In 1935 the attendance at these functions became so large that they had to be held in the Music Hall.

Frank H. Gerrodette, the first director, entered on his duties in June, 1896, but resigned on September 19, 1896.

In 1898 W. J. Holland (1848-1932) was appointed director, and under his leadership the Museum moved rapidly forward to a position of importance among similar institutions in this country. A clergyman, educator, and scientist, he was an individual of many parts, one of the last specimens of the Renaissance ideal of the "complete" or unspecialized man. He was an entomologist of note, and his collection of Lepidoptera, deposited in the Museum, was a notable one. Much interested in paleontology, Dr. Holland guided work in that field, for which the Museum was especially noted, in the early years of this century. He retired in 1922.

The 1890's and the first decade of the twentieth century were the golden day of the capitalist world, and Andrew Carnegie was prodigal of the millions in his coffers. In those days the Museum often profited from his benefactions, and so many donations were coming in from other quarters that the Museum was overcrowded soon after it opened. The founder had also set up endowments for both the Museum and the

Fine Arts Department, which were administered by the Carnegie Institute. The actual running expenses of the Museum were, therefore, taken care of, but the matter of physical expansion became of prime importance. The new urn was already in place, but there was not room for the tree to grow, so it was necessary for the container to be enlarged.

The presence of the great dinosaur skeletons that the Museum had acquired constituted one of the most compelling reasons for expansion. In such a brief study as this one can select only the most important and dramatic of its collections for mention, and no doubt the paleontological group at Carnegie would claim pride of place. Archeology had overwhelmingly captured the imagination of the nineteenth-century public, and all kinds of excavations, from the site of Troy to the dinosaur quarry in Utah, were looked upon with a wonder and fascination that seem a little naive to a later generation. What marvels would the earth yield next?

Not the least awed and interested of the spectators watching the emergence of this sunken world was Andrew Carnegie, who for many years beginning in 1899 gave the Museum a special fund for field work in paleontology. Every year expeditions worked in the Far West—Wyoming, Colorado, Nebraska, and Utah—and some notable finds were uncovered that made the Museum famous as a center of such research. *Diplodocus carnegiei*, discovered in Wyoming in 1889, was the earliest as it was one of the most spectacular trophies of these great dinosaur-hunting parties. The donor caused ten plaster casts of it to be made, which he presented to national museums from Russia to the Argentine.

The ancient historic past, as it was gradually unfolding through Egyptian excavation, also claimed the interest of the general public, and there was even a Pittsburgh branch of the Egypt Exploration Fund whose members contributed to the local collections. Andrew Carnegie, like many millionaires of the period, traveled in Egypt, and he donated to the Museum several objects, including a mummy and the wooden soul boat of Sesostris III, which was so large that is could not be taken into the old building. While the new Museum was being constructed, the boat was placed in a nearby shed, and when construction had advanced far enough, it was hoisted through the wall of the interior court, where it was placed under a temporary covering until the outer walls could be built. Dramatically lighted, it now presides over the Museum's Ancient Near East Hall.

The three years during which the additions were under construction were a time of trial for the Museum, since many of the collections could not be shown. The new building, opened in 1907, had a plenitude of rooms and courts for exhibition purposes, and larger and more convenient laboratories, storerooms, and offices. However much the style of the installations may have changed, the general format of the place has not been altered because no additions have been made to the building since it was opened.

A large Edwardian quietude pervaded the stately spaciousness of the galleries of that day. There was a good deal of marble, mahogany, and brass; great expanses of plate glass shone from display cases and the ample windows. The luminous marble elegance of the great stair hall prepared the way for the long range of rooms on the east side of the structure. Despite the Puritan plainness of architecture, there lingered about these wide spaces an almost regal tone, a muted echo of their palatial inspiration. The Edwardian galleries in general represented a sort of transition between nineteenth-century display techniques and the simplified, rigorously ordered, and artfully presented methods of today.

The Gallery of Useful Arts, (now housing the conservation exhibit), which displayed the Heinz ivories and the DuPuy collection of objects of art, led into the Fossil Halls and the two-storied Hall of the Dinosaurs with a kind of grand inconsequence, an aristocratic disdain of the easy or artful approach to culture. Here were selections from the wealth of the ages, fragments of the history of the earth all properly arranged and labled; this was an unadorned display presented forthrightly in the full light of day, and the spectator could take it or leave it. For the most part, he took it, even if his feet hurt him occasionally and his eye became a trifle glazed.

At the southeastern end of the Museum, the presentation of the exhibits was a little more popular, rather less formal, but there was still a good deal of marble and plate glass. The mounted specimens in the Hall of Mammals were—and are—beloved, particularly a group representing a camel driver attacked by Barbary lions. This dramatic and fascinating example of Victorian taxidermy, first exhibited in the Paris Exposition of 1869, has recently been refurbished.

Frederic S. Webster, who was chief preparator at the Museum from 1897 to 1908 and the outstanding bird taxidermist of his time, was a pioneer in the development of habitat groups and, while at the Museum, made some notable contributions to exhibition technique.

The most dramatic objects in the Museum's collections remain today, as in those early days. *Diplodocus carnegiei, Apatosaurus louisae, Stegosaurus,* and *Tyrannosaurus rex.* The reconstructed skeletons of these great creatures, once naked to the light of the Edwardian day, are now presented to the contemporary public in the full panoply of the most advanced display technique, but the tremendous drama of these monsters is implicit in the bones themselves that arch like ruined osseous cathedrals above the museum-goer's head.

One of the art galleries, 1908

A view of a recent "International", an exhibit of contemporary art
from throughout the world held triennially.

V

THE OLD RESTORED

The First Art Galleries Reappear

ART GALLERIES by reason of their size rarely vanish, but the visitor to the Carnegie Library of Pittsburgh may walk into a suite of rooms that had almost disappeared, only to be recently recovered. The dismantling of the Carnegie Library School installations in 1962 revealed again the three galleries where the first International art exhibitions were held, beginning in 1896. These high and spacious halls, with their coved ceilings and Classical architraves and cornices, were part of the original Carnegie Library building dedicated in 1895, and they have a certain importance as the first real public art galleries in the city of Pittsburgh.

It is difficult now to imagine the pride Pittsburghers once felt for their new cultural center — its quattrocento corridors, the Italian towers of the Music Hall, the huge, vaulted Reference Room praised as the "grand gold hall", and the three wide galleries lined with the more than three hundred paintings of the opening exhibition of 1895. The visitor today, however, faced with the great, recently painted rooms that now house the Music Division and the Pennsylvania Room of the Central Library, may well consider these galleries as they once were, lined with tightly packed canvases and thronged with turn-of-the-century art lovers.

The opening exhibition of 1895, consisting of European works mostly owned in Pittsburgh, was so successful that Andrew Carnegie decided to make provision for an annual exhibition that would bring a wide selection of modern art to Pittsburgh. The first International opened in these galleries in 1896, and it was succeeded by seven more. The ninth and tenth exhibitions were held in a temporary building erected at the side of the Music Hall, and the eleventh exhibition of 1907 was held in the present galleries of the Museum of Art.

The original galleries were thus the birthplace of what is still probably the most important exhibition of modern art in America. The skylights that once cast down a pale, intense light on the heavily populated walls have been painted over, but now that the partitions have been removed from these rooms it is possible to recall them as they were in the brief years of their glory. One's imagination readily fills in the intent, late-Victorian gallery-goers peering, among the potted palms and the steam heat, at the crowded, expansive canvases.

Entrance to Museum

Index